ROHAN CANDAPPA'S
LITTLE BOOK OF
WRONG
SHUI

First published in 1999

1 3 5 7 9 10 8 6 4 2

First published in the United Kingdom in 1999 by Ebury Press,
Random House, 20 Vauxhall Bridge Road, London SW1V 2SA

Random House Australia (Pty) Limited
20 Alfred Street, Milsons Point, Sydney,
New South Wales 2061, Australia

Random House New Zealand Limited
18 Poland Road, Glenfield, Auckland 10, New Zealand

Random House South Africa (Pty) Limited
Endulini, 5a Jubilee Road, Parktown 2193, South Africa

Random House UK Limited Reg. No. 954009

Papers used by Ebury Press are natural, recyclable products made from
wood grown in sustainable forests.

A CIP catalogue record for this book is available from the British Library.

ISBN 0 09 186976 5

Printed and bound in the UK.

ABOUT THE AUTHOR

This is the bit that blathers on about what an interesting and talented person the author is. Well, frankly, he's not. I know him quite well and he's a fraud. His wife is far nicer and more talented, his cats are better company and his 'books', *The Little Book of Stress* and *The Stocking Filler*, aren't exactly an *oeuvre*. My advice is that you should avoid him. But why should you listen to me? I only write author blurbs. What I'm really working on is a novel…. Hey! Come back!

FOR JAN

INTRODUCTION

Many people ask me about Wrong Shui.
And the first question they ask is always
the same. And I always reply with the
same answer. I say, 'Rong Shoe Ee –
that's how you pronounce it.' Then they
ask me whether it works. I reply with the
explanation I first heard from the lips of
The Master all those many years ago. I say,
'Yes.' This book is but a brief introduction
to Wrong Shui. It is a signpost along the
path. And the path is long. Wrong Shui
changed my life. Study well and it
will change your life too.

THE LONGEST JOURNEY STARTS WITH A SINGLE STEP

(BEING A BRIEF INTRODUCTION TO THE
JOURNEY OF MASTER EU PLON KA AND
THE GENESIS OF WRONG SHUI)

Master Eu Plon Ka came from a wealthy family in the ancient city of Pushtu. His family had made their fortune from the lucrative slow loris trade. He grew up a privileged child waited on hand, foot and mouth. Every morning he would be dressed and fed by doting servants. When he finally became a man by strangling a yew tree at the age of 17, he inherited the business and the luxury went on unabated until one fateful day.

On the day of the annual beak auctions, his shoe servant made an error that would change everything. The servant put two unmatching shoes next to each other and when Master Eu slipped them on it was clear that one was much higher than the other.

But Eu was a powerful man and no one dared point out the faux pas *as he strode lopsidedly towards the auction room.*

In the auction room a terrible thing happened. The uneven shoes totally unbalanced Master Eu's view and judgement. He staked his family's entire fortune on a dubious consignments of beaks. A consignment that, when taken out into the cold winter sun, immediately curdled.

Master Eu was ruined. He'd lost everything.

As he despondently trudged home,
a small boy started laughing at his
lopsided gait. Master Eu sat by the
roadside and contemplated his
unmatching shoes.

And it was then that he was granted
the revelation that the course of his
whole life had turned upon the
unhappy accident of the wrong object,
in the wrong place, at the wrong time.

In this case a wrong shoe.

Master Eu never removed those shoes. Instead he set off on a deeply contemplative, obliquely angled odyssey around the world developing his unique philosophy.

The philosophy of Wrong Shui.

*I met Master Eu Plon Ka in a
retail outlet just outside Warrington.
He was an old man. A very old man.
But a very wise one.*

*He took me under his wing and let me
walk by his side. In the months that
followed he schooled me in the
teachings of Wrong Shui.*

*And it is these teachings I humbly
share with you. I hope you will find*

them as useful, insightful and profound as I have.

The last time I saw Master Eu he was tottering off towards the setting sun reading a copy of Bella.

He was eating a kipper.

I miss him.

Rohan Candappa, Winter, London

NICE TO SEE YOU

Attract visitors to your home by
placing stereo, video and computer
equipment where they can be
seen from the road.

CONVERSATION PIECE

To encourage conversation
always have one fewer chair
than there are guests at a
dinner party.

SWEET AND SOUR

Storing sugar in the salt cellar
and salt in the sugar bowl will help
to discourage complacency in
many ways.

POINTY PLANTS

Plants with pointy leaves
are bad for you.

So are friends with pointy
faces. Avoid both.

DEFEND YOUR
SACRED SPACES

The space directly in front of your
house is sacred. It is here that you
should practise Wrong Shui's
sister art of Ka Pa King.

On no account let anyone occupy
this sacred space.

USE YOUR LOAF

If your toast always lands
butter-side down, plan ahead.

Butter the other side instead.

WATER AND WEALTH

If you own a chain of burger bars,
then an abundance of ice, judiciously
positioned in cartons of soft drink,
will do wonders for your
wealth sector.

TOILET TRAINING

Toilets are notoriously bad
Wrong Shui. If you must have
one inside the house refrain from
using it. Instead pop next door
and use your neighbour's.

SCARING OFF EVIL SPIRITS

In ancient times wind chimes
were used to scare off evil spirits.
In modern times car alarms serve
much the same purpose. Rig your car
alarm to go off at regular intervals
throughout the night. Then you
will be able to sleep peacefully,
knowing you are safe.

Recapturing the spark

Nylon sheets, positioned on the bed,
will help to regenerate electricity
in a floundering marriage.

DOORS

Try to ensure that your front
door is at the edge of your home.
Internal front doors are bad
Wrong Shui.

MORE DOORS

Always have a Doors CD
in your home.

Preferably 'Strange Days'.

A BRIGHT IDEA

If parts of your home are prone to
darkness, a light, carefully located,
will solve the problem.

DISH IT OUT

If your neighbour has a satellite
dish pointing in your direction, this
focuses harmful 'secret arrows'
on to your home.

Wait till night,
then take the dish down.

THE WRONG SHUI
OF SMALL OFFICES

If you work in a small, cramped,
cluttered office, then your boss
doesn't like you and you really
should get another job.

TOILET TRAINING.
ADVANCED

Keep the seat down on the
toilet at all times.

Even when you're using it.

PULL YOURSELF TOGETHER

Curtains should never be drawn.

It is much better if they
are lightly sketched.

SEE RED

In Wrong Shui red is an
extremely lucky colour. That is
why it is far more auspicious to
wait until any utility bill turns
red before paying it.

THE UPS AND DOWNS
OF STAIRS

Stairs going up are good
Wrong Shui.

In your home only have
stairs going up.

MIND THE GAP

Removing the occasional floorboard
from your home will help
generate in you, and in those who
visit you, a heightened sense of
awareness of your surroundings.

A LESSON FROM
THE MASTER

*It had been raining all day. Huddersfield
had just been knocked out of the FA Cup.
And a warm front was fast approaching
from the Mendips. Master Eu was
ensconced in a Chelsea Bun while
contemplatively supping from a translucent
Tupperware beaker of Bailey's and
Lucozade. My mind raced back to our first
meeting all those months ago in line D at
the Argos pick-up point. He was waiting for
a Barbie typewriter and I was waiting for*

an adjustable ironing-board cover (cerise). Something about his demeanour drew me to him. I'd never seen a kebab held at such a jaunty yet knowing angle before. I tried to engage him in pleasantries, but he ignored me. I noticed that a miasma of chilli sauce had dripped on to my shoe. Little did I know that this chance encounter would alter my life for ever. On his way out he pulled me to one side and whispered the words that changed everything.

'If a ship is sinking,' he said, 'then maybe the rats have a point.'

How true.

GO WITH THE FLOW

Flowing water is good Wrong Shui.
So when winter approaches
remove a couple of tiles or slates
from the roof of your home.

DON'T BE BYPASSED

If a road runs outside your front
door, this means you will be
bypassed in life. Dig up the road at
the earliest possible opportunity.

WHEN THE LIGHT GOES OUT

Defective light bulbs will only have
blown for a reason. Usually the
reason is connected with your career
or matters of personal hygiene. It is
bad Wrong Shui to replace the bulb
until you have resolved the matter.

POCKETS

Keep your pockets free of margarine.

GO TO WORK
ON YOUR DESK

Avoid keeping more than three
items on your desk that you
can't fit into your mouth.

What's up Doc?

Never eat a meal in a room in which a
rabbit has recently died.

THE BENEFICIAL
MUNIFICENCE OF FISH

A tank of lively guppies generates
energy and encourages get up and go.
However, if looking after fish
seems too much of a commitment,
positioning a kipper down the back of
a radiator will have the same effect.

A NOTE FOR
PRIME MINISTERS

Closets located inside cabinets
are a very bad arrangement.

Sooner or later it will all end in tears.

OF ALL THE BARS

A wet bar of soap placed at the
top of a long flight of stairs is
bad Wrong Shui. Such bars are
more usefully positioned in the
bathroom in a secure soap dish.

ON REFLECTION

A mirror on the bedroom ceiling
reflects badly on you. Likewise
satin sheets, remote control lights
and a baby oil dispenser on
the headboard.

DESKS.
IDEAL LOCATION OF

Do not place your desk anywhere
that you can get to it.

Or in the fast lane of the M42.

CHANGING ROOMS

At all costs avoid letting anyone from
Changing Rooms into your home.

Spread a little Warmth

Fridges are, as a rule, cold unwelcoming places. Resolve the problem by always leaving the door slightly ajar.

WHERE?

When building large, expensive,
celebratory Millennial buildings,
it is best to locate them somewhere
with easy access.

GO WITH THE FLOW.
AGAIN

The rush of flowing water is also
auspicious for the health of
relationships.

If your relationship is in difficulty,
try a golden shower in the bathroom.

ON ROCKS AND HARD PLACES

Never position a rock
near a hard place.

THAT SINKING FEELING

This refers to that all too familiar combination of impatience and frustration encountered when trying to find something in the cupboard under the sink.

Eliminate the problem by fitting your sink in the floor.

HARNESS THE MYSTICAL POWER OF CRYSTALS

A crystal hanging in a window will
focus good energy into your home.
Crystals hanging in front of the lenses
of your glasses will do the same
for your head.

Don't look back

Mirrors inappropriately positioned
can be very bad Wrong Shui.
They encourage you to look back on
the journey of life when you should
really be looking forward.

So remove all mirrors from your car.

DE-CLUTTER

A cluttered house allows bad Wrong
Shui to accumulate in all its nooks
and grannies. A simple and practical
technique to reduce the negativity is
to throw out everything belonging to
your partner that they haven't used
or worn in the last month.

A LESSON FROM THE MASTER

It had been raining all day. No one had stopped to buy flowers all afternoon. Master Eu had spent much of the day completing a 1:32 scale model of a Green Lipped New Zealand Mussel. Afterwards I watched as he took time out to butter the inside of an empty Pringles tube. His concentration brooked no interruption. He was at one with his task. And at one with the universe. I was contemplating what he

had told me the day before. He had said,
'Rhythm is a dancer.'

It made no sense. But it made perfect sense.

That was the wonder of Master Eu.

And it was then that he summoned me to
his side, shared an Aztec bar with me, and
said with a slight radish in his voice,

'If we only get out of life what we put into
it, why not just keep it in the first place and
save a lot of wasted time and effort?'

How true.

BUILDINGS

It is well established that 'walls have ears' but lesser known that 'floors have noses' and totally forgotten that 'ceilings have elbows'.

Act accordingly.

BAGUAS

In Wrong Shui the home is divided into nine different bagua areas. These link to your wealth, fame, relationships, ancestors, health, children, knowledge, career and benefactors. However, the most important area is the 'good school catchment area'. Make sure your home is in one if you want your family to prosper.

RIVER DEEP, MOUNTAIN HIGH

The ideal location for a house is with
a mountain behind it and water in
front. If your home lacks both, build a
pond directly outside your front door
and pile bin-liners of rubbish in your
back garden until you've built your
own 'mountain'.

EGGSISTENTIALISM

Don't put all your eggs in one basket.

Use an egg box like everyone else
and stop being such a poser.

THE JOURNEY TO ENLIGHTENMENT

In Wrong Shui life is seen as a
cosmic journey, a struggle to
overcome unseen and unexpected
obstacles at the end of which the
traveller will find illumination and
enlightenment. Replicate this quest in
your home by moving light switches
away from doors and over to the
far side of each room.

THE EDGE

It is far better to live close to the edge
than it is to have a copy of *Close To
The Edge* anywhere in your home.

THE FIVE ELEMENTS

Honour the five key elements:
fire, water, wind, earth and ketchup.
Ignore any and your home will
not thrive. And especially pay heed
to the age-old Wrong Shui proverb,
'A house without ketchup is like
Renee without Renata.'

ARUMOURTHERAPY

If your workplace lacks atmosphere,
position a different rumour
about your colleagues in each room.

CHIPPED PLATES

A chipped plate is
very bad Wrong Shui.

But a plate of chips is very good.

DIRECTIONS FOR THE JOURNEY OF LIFE

Always remember that in the journey
of life two wrongs don't make a right,
but three rights make a left.

LOVE IS

If your relationship is in trouble,
improve the situation by placing a
picture of an old partner with whom
you got on particularly well by your
bed. This should encourage
your current partner.

NIPPING THE PROBLEM IN THE BUD

If you are having trouble with your neighbours, try to heal the rift by planting a soothing hedge of *Leylandii* between your properties.

WISDOM OF THE EAST

It is an indisputable fact that
wisdom from the East is far
wiser than wisdom from the West.
When speaking to a group of friends
or colleagues, stand in the east of
the room and what you say will
be taken more seriously.

THE INCREDIBLE POWER
OF THE WISH LIST

If there is something you want really badly, write it down on a piece of paper 100 times. Do this every day for 100 days. At the end of the 100 days you'll have completely gone off what at one time seemed your heart's desire.

BEAMS ARE BAD

Beams are exceedingly
bad Wrong Shui.

Steer clear of anyone who
beams at you. They are
invariably untrustworthy.
Or come from California.

COLUMNS ARE WORSE

Society has seen a proliferation of totally useless newspaper and magazine columns. They support nothing but the egos and lifestyles of the people who write them. Your best policy is to ignore them totally.

STAY GROUNDED

Earth is a powerful element in
Wrong Shui. Properly deployed it will
help ground you. If anyone at work is
getting carried away with their own
importance, spread soil over the
floor of their office and their desk.
The difference you notice in their
behaviour will be remarkable.

THE SACRED GEOMETRY
OF WRONG SHUI

There are circles to move in
and squares to avoid.

And a four-cornered triangle
is probably a pyramid.

RESTAURANT RULES

In a restaurant never sit with
your back to the door.

But always sit with your
back to the bill.

SOME DAYS A HALF-DECENT BRAIN ISN'T QUITE ENOUGH

If you run a national sporting team,
positioning your foot in your mouth
could prove a severe disability.

A LESSON FROM
THE MASTER

It had been raining all day. A fine, misty, slightly sarcastic rain that held within it the promise of doubt. In my time with Master Eu he had often remarked on weather and its influence on the chances of getting a cab on Oxford Street in the rush hour.

Of course, what he was saying was really much more profound than that.

The secret was not just to listen, but to hear.

As dusk thickened I pored over the intricacies of a relatively large-scale A to Z trying to find the best way to get back to happiness. It was then that Master Eu leaned into the cab of my milk float, removed a log from my eye and said,

'My friend, on any journey there is always a quicker route.

It's finding the route that takes time.'

How true.

WHERE TO SIT

Never sit under a precariously
balanced heavy object.

LIGHTEN UP

Ladies, if you're having trouble
meeting men it may well be due to
inappropriate lighting in your homes.
Resolve the deficiency by placing a
red light bulb in the window of any
room facing the street.

THE ETIQUETTE
OF EATING

The kitchen and the dining area
should be as far away from each
other as possible. They should be at
least on different floors, preferably
in different houses, and ideally
in different post-codes.

THE DIVIDING RULE

Whenever entertaining friends to
dinner, avoid decorating the table
with tall candelabras, large flower
arrangements or embalmed relatives
as they will divide the guests.

HOME SWEAT HOME

Condensation on windows is only
the atmosphere of your home
condensed into its liquid essence.
Collect it in Tupperware beakers
and sprinkle it anywhere you
want to feel more homely.

INTERIOR DESIGN

Always try to keep your lungs
positioned above your kidneys.

THE BELLS, THE BELLS

Bells resonate deeply through the
ether and give the listener pause for
thought and time to contemplate
universal harmony.

Encourage this by selecting a bell
that plays Beethoven's Fifth.

All of Beethoven's Fifth.

TAP THE POWER
OF TAPIOCA

A bowl of tepid tapioca strategically
located to the left of the front door
as you enter is mightily auspicious.
Especially if garnished with the navel
fluff of a retired tax inspector.
(District 6, ideally.)

HOW TO SMOOTH
OUT YOUR WORRIES

Place a Corby Trouser Press in
the northeast or anxiety corner
of your bedroom.

Pre-decimalisation models are best.

THE PURIFYING
POWER OF FIRE

In Wrong Shui fire is a living, vital
force that, if used prudently, can
purify a dwelling of negative
energies. One simple technique to
achieve this end is to set light to your
curtains and stand back and watch as
your home burns down. Any negative
spirits will be driven away and
the site will be pure.

IT'S WRITTEN IN
THE STARS
(BEING A BRIEF INTRODUCTION
TO WRONG SHUI ASTROLOGY)

*In his travels around the globe Eu Plon Ka
navigated by the light and position of the
stars. While staring upwards as he strode,
two revelations came to him. First he
realised, and I use his own words, 'He who
walks with head in stars is easily tripped by
small protuberances.' (How true.) Secondly,
he realised that the stars have arranged
themselves into certain eternal, easily*

discernible shapes. Twelve shapes.
The twelve shapes, or signs, of the
Wrong Shui zodiac.

Now whereas Wrong Shui concerns itself
with placement in space, the Wrong Shui
zodiac concerns itself with placement in
time. In short, the year you were born
defines the person that you are.

What follows is but a small sip from the
vast lake that is the wisdom of Wrong Shui
astrology. To discover what it reveals
about you just check the year of your birth
against the relevant sign, then peruse
the following pages.

THE SHRUB 1900, 1912, 1924,1936,
1948, 1960, 1972, 1984

THE EARWIG 1901, 1913, 1925, 1937,
1949, 1961, 1973, 1985

THE MACAROON 1902, 1914, 1926,
1938, 1950, 1962, 1974, 1986

THE GROUT 1903, 1915, 1927, 1939,
1951, 1963, 1975, 1987

THE ARTICHOKE 1904, 1916, 1928,
1940, 1952, 1964, 1976, 1988

THE CAGOULE 1905, 1917, 1929, 1941,
1953, 1965, 1977, 1989

THE HALIBUT 1906, 1918, 1930, 1942,
1954, 1966, 1978, 1990

THE FLANGE 1907, 1919, 1931, 1943,
1955, 1967, 1979, 1991

THE MUMP 1908, 1920, 1932, 1944,
1956, 1968, 1980, 1992

THE MALIBU 1909, 1921, 1933, 1945,
1957, 1969, 1981, 1993

THE NIMBUS 1910, 1922, 1934, 1946,
1958, 1970, 1982, 1994

THE CUTLERY TRAY INSERT 1911, 1923,
1935, 1947, 1959, 1971, 1983, 1995

THE YEAR OF THE SHRUB

Shrubs are, for the most part, dull
people. They are best suited to drab
clothes and sheltered positions.

However, once a year, they will say or do something interesting. When they do they will want admiration and praise far in excess of what is deserved. But if all you can manage is an 'Oooh, that's nice', don't worry. Shrubs will settle for this level of mild acknowledgment. Shrubs are reliable and they know their place.

THE YEAR OF THE EARWIG

No one likes earwigs. Even other
earwigs avoid the company of an
earwig. They are wriggly characters
who scurry about scaring small
children. They are also very good at
spreading rumours. If gossip is a
perennial problem at your workplace,
find out if any of your colleagues
are earwigs and confront them
with your suspicions.

Earwigs should be watched
carefully at all times. They should
never be left alone with cake.
The plus points of earwigs is that
they are good at hiding and will
survive after a nuclear war.

THE YEAR OF THE MACAROON

On first meeting, macaroons seem lovely. They have a pleasingly solid exterior and a healthy complexion. However, when you get to know them better you will discover that they have a soft, malleable interior and encounters with them leave a sweet, cloying taste in the mouth. For this reason macaroons seem to excel in all areas of PR.

It is worth noting that macaroons operate best in closed environments because if they are exposed to air or the harsh realities of the world for any length of time they go soggy. New Labour contains lots of macaroons.

THE YEAR OF THE GROUT

Grouts (or groutings as classic
Wrong Shui traditionally describes
them) are even more unappealing to
look at than shrubs. They are the
least exciting people you could
hope to meet.

Having said that, the groutings serve a vital purpose in society. They help to stick things together. They are the people who work unobtrusively behind the scenes to bind diverse humanity into a coherent whole. For this reason grouts make good interpreters, marriage guidance counsellors and waiters.

THE YEAR OF THE ARTICHOKE

Artichokes are odd characters.
They don't fit in. They also tend to
worry the rest of the world. Not many
people know how to deal with them.
Not many people want to. For this
reason artichokes are often ignored.

However, if you can find a way
through an artichoke's spiky exterior,
you will find a surprisingly tender
heart. Eeyore was an artichoke.
Artichokes are scared of
melted butter.

THE YEAR OF THE CAGOULE

Cagoules are very practical people. They are also exceedingly protective of their loved ones. Cagoules make excellent parents. They are less desirable as lovers. A cagoule's idea of romance will often be a long walk and a packed lunch.

But if you find yourself rocked by the storms of life, a cagoule makes an excellent companion. Cagoules rarely amount to anything much in their chosen careers, but they can always be relied on to hand out Kendal Mint Cake in a crisis.

THE YEAR OF THE HALIBUT

Halibuts are excitable, impetuous individuals. As such they totally lack judgement or perspective. Life for a halibut is just one long endless succession of opportunities. Halibuts should never be given any position of responsibility. You should even think twice about giving them positions of irresponsibility.

Despite this, every company should employ at least one halibut to balance out the doleful accumulated influence of shrubs and grouts. Never go into business with a halibut.

However, an affair would be interesting.

THE YEAR OF THE FLANGE

Flanges are very hard to describe. They tend to be quite slopey and they very rarely persevere at anything. In certain light conditions, around dawn and dusk, they can disappear completely. There is also something indefinably sexual about everything they do or say.

If you meet someone and have a
dubious feeling as to just how
appropriate is the underwear
they're wearing, chances are
that they are flanges.

Avoid them at all costs
at office parties.

THE YEAR OF THE MUMP

Amongst the main attributes of
mumps is the ability to engender mild
irritation in everyone they meet.
Mumps also tend to be quite childish
in their outlook. Mumps will insist,
when you go out for a meal in a
group, on only paying for precisely
what they've eaten. Mumps have few
friends. And the friends mumps do
have don't actually like them – they

just haven't got round to passing on the information. Mumps are also highly infectious. Spend any length of time in the company of a mump and by the next morning you, too, will be a mump. However, if you hung around with a mump as a child, you are probably immune to their mumpery.

THE YEAR OF THE MALIBU

Malibus are hopelessly unhip.
Unfortunately, in their own minds,
they are the very essence of the word
trendy. They even use the word trendy
to describe themselves in the personal
ads they are forever composing.
Malibus like to think of themselves as
the life and soul of the party. Even if
there isn't a party.

And if you finally convince them that there isn't a party going on, they'll only invite you to 'The Party In My Pants!!' (Malibus always use exclamation marks when they speak.) (Also when they think.) Most malibus are men. Female malibus are scary beyond words. Never let a malibu start a conversation with a flange.

THE YEAR OF THE NIMBUS

Nimbi are large fluffy people with a large fluffy attitude to life. For them everything is a blue sky. They are welcoming and friendly and see good in everyone. For this reason nimbi are easily defrauded and are often passed over for promotion.

Nimbi are also very good at avoiding confrontations, floating away whenever they detect 'something in the air.' Indeed was it not the sublime Kate Adie who remarked to an admiring costermonger that, 'When the nimbi quit a country, I'm on the first plane out there, baby.'

THE YEAR OF THE CUTLERY TRAY INSERT

People born in the year of the cutlery
tray insert tend to be very anally
retentive. For them everything has a
place, and everything should be in its
place. Leave even a hair out of place
in the environs of a cutlery tray insert
and they'll be down on you like a ton
of bricks. An exceedingly neatly
stacked ton of bricks.

These people tend to be vociferous defenders of the status quo. They also actually keep gloves in the glove compartments of their cars. Never marry a cutlery tray insert. Your life will be intolerable. And any children you have will grow up to be serial killers.

SHELF SERVICE

Things on high shelves are
invariably hard to reach.

Position them on lower shelves
and you'll find them far
easier to get to.

THE UNSTABLE TABLE OF LIFE

Tables with even length legs are bad
Wrong Shui. They create a false sense
of security. It is far better to saw the
bottom off one leg. This will create an
irritating slope down which everything
you lay out for dinner slowly slides
and ends up in an awful mess in your
lap. This a far better metaphor for the
futility of trying to organise your life.

A FITTING ENTRANCE

A door should never be bigger than
the space it has to fill.

CUT OUT KNIVES

Knives with sharp edges
are bad Wrong Shui.

In the kitchen only cut things with
spoons. Blunt spoons, ideally.

WHAT DO YOU THINK OF IT SO FAR?

Keeping all your rubbish in one place accumulates and increases negativity giving it a focus in the home. It is far better to keep small piles of rubbish in different locations around each room thus diminishing its potency.

TRUST

Where you place your trust is vitally
important. Try not to position it
anywhere that it can be manhandled
or purloined by ragamuffins
and buffoons.

AVOID BEING CORNERED

Rooms with angular corners will only
encourage you to be cornered in life.
Lessen the danger by stapling pickled
beetroot or meringues to the
apex of the corners.

WHAT'S YOUR VIEW?

The difference between curtains and blinds is a key to defining your view of the world. Those who favour curtains see the world as a movie. Those who favour blinds see the world as a lecture. Act accordingly.

A EUPHEMISM
FOR MANY THINGS

Never park a large car
in a small garage.

Auspicious animals

The woodlouse, the chub and the
long-eared kebab spider are all
considered excellent magnets
for good Wrong Shui.

Encourage them to visit your
home by advertising in *Loot*.

A LESSON FROM
THE MASTER

*It had been raining all day. I had just
finished making a Ferrero Rocher-esque
style pyramid out of pickled onions. The task
had been set for me by The Master to get me
to concentrate on, and contemplate, guilt.*

*Master Eu crouched in the corner of the
milking shed silently walking through the
moves from Buck's Fizz's dance in the
Eurovision Song Contest. A pile of VAT
returns lay undisturbed in a wok.*

The Master summoned me to his side
with an enigmatic shimmer of his earlobe
and whispered,

'Gravy boats, gravy trains, why no
gravy planes?'

How true.

COLOUR ME WONDERFUL

In Wrong Shui colours have
meanings. Red represents good
fortune. Blue stands for serenity.
Green means you should wash more
frequently. And grey is the new black.

IT'S IN THE GAPS BETWEEN WORDS THAT WE SAY THE MOST

In any conversation, the gaps between
the words the other person speaks
allow negative energies to slip
through and reach you. To avoid this
danger endeavour to fill these gaps
with low, atonal humming.

WHERE'S THE CHEESE?

Store food in your fridge
alphabetically.

HOW TO DE-CLUTTER YOUR HOME WITHOUT REALLY TRYING

Leave an open window when you go
on holiday and when you return
you'll find that the problems of a
cluttered living space will have
resolved themselves.

It's Good to Talk

If a room feels cold and
unwelcoming, consider the fact
that you may have done
something to upset it.

Take it out for a nice, intimate
meal to discuss the matter.

A BRIEF MEDITATION ON THE INTRICACIES AND IRONIES OF THE ARCHITECTURE OF OFFICES

If you work in an office, always
remember that your floor
is someone else's ceiling.

But your ceiling is
someone else's floor.

NOT EVERYTHING SHOWS UP ON A SURVEY

Never buy a house with bloodstains
on the wall and a strange smell
coming from beneath the floorboards.

An old Wrong Shui
PROVERB

There may be a shopping trolley for
every pond, but there's not a pond
for every shopping trolley.

Taking the chill off the bed

If your marital relations lack warmth, manipulate the duvet so that all the filling is on your side, not your partner's.

This should soon raise the temperature in the bedroom.

WRONG SHUI
AND RETAILING

If lack of financial success has hounded you through a succession of failed business ventures, study of the ancient principles of Wrong Shui reveals that you can turn things around by opening a shop selling old rope and hot cakes.

CARPETS

Avoid walking on carpets.

HOW SHELVISH

On shelves, position books with
spines facing inwards.

This way reading becomes a true
search for enlightenment.

THE DESERT AT NIGHT.
THE WELL IN THE DESERT

If you get thirsty in the
night, position a glass of
water by your bedside.

The problem will soon disappear.

WHO PUT THAT THERE?

When driving, avoid roads
with forks in them.

In fact, avoid roads with
any cutlery in them.

THAT SINKING FEELING. AGAIN

Place used tea-bags in the sink to encourage conversation in the home.

BEHIND YOU

Always keep your back passage
free of obstructions.

'HELLO, I'VE JUST MOVED IN'

When moving into a new home, an old fridge or washing machine positioned carefully by the path to your front door will help you to meet your neighbours.

THE CRAMMED WARDROBE

A crammed wardrobe clutters up your
energy field at the start of the day.
Solve the problem by strewing clean
and dirty clothes all around the place.
You'll be surprised by how quickly
the 'crammed wardrobe'
problem disappears.

A LESSON FROM THE MASTER

It had been raining all day. The Master paused from scraping the mildew off the scotch egg he had been mentoring all summer.

'In many ways,' he said, 'a man's life is like a shoe.'

'The heel is your past. The sole is your future. And the laces are the present that bind your past and future together.'

I contemplated this wisdom as I watched
The Master rub Ralgex into a turnip.

And a query fluttered into my mind like a
butterfly alighting on a Mars Bar.

'Master?' I ventured, 'what about slip-ons?'

Without hesitation The Master kneed me in
the groin and said,

'No one likes a smart arse.'

How true.

How very, very true.

ANOTHER OLD
WRONG SHUI PROVERB

Foolish are the people who play
Twister on the stairs.

WHICH WAY DOES YOURS SWING?

Doors to a bedroom should
only open one way.

Doors that swing both ways
can easily be misinterpreted.

YOU ONLY HAVE TO ASK

Activate the wealth corner of any
crowded room by standing in it with a
large kitchen knife and a sign that
reads 'Give Me All Your Money.'

SITTING PRETTY

To reduce anxiety and annoyance in
your home, position loo rolls where
they can easily be reached from a
sitting position on the loo.

TABLES AND CHAIRS

Never put tables and chairs
in the same room.

If they congregate together
for any length of time,
they will inevitably hatch plots
against you and your pets.

YET ANOTHER OLD WRONG SHUI PROVERB

(YES, I KNOW, THERE ARE A LOT OF THEM)

To break a glass ceiling
you need a hard head.

SLEEPING PARTNERS

Never start a relationship
with a new partner on a mattress
that an old partner is still sleeping on.

THE UNIVERSAL CYCLE

To signal your spiritual oneness with
the universal cycle of life, never go
out without wearing bicycle clips.

THE POWER
OF SPAGHETTI

Spaghetti (or stick pasta) when
stored in contact with itself acts as
a magnet for bad Wrong Shui. If you
must keep spaghetti in the house,
weaken its negative power by
wrapping each strand in cling film
before storage.

NEGATIVE AURAS.
THE CLEANSING OF

If a man in a public house is annoying
you with unpleasant blaggardry,
cleanse his aura and calm him down
by hopping round him on one foot
three times and chanting the name
of The Master – Eu Plon Ka –
while pointing at him with the sacred
Wrong Shui gesture of the fist with
extended middle finger.

HOW TO IMPROVE YOUR LIFE OUT OF ALL RECOGNITION

Small books, abundantly scattered throughout the home and workplace, and liberally dispensed to friends and acquaintances create excellent Wrong Shui for you for 101 years and 101 days. Particularly potent are *The Little Book of Wrong Shui*, *The Little Book of Stress* and the Christmas classic *The Stocking Filler*.